WISDOM FROM MY FATHER'S PORCH

(A Guide for Young Black Men)

Dr. Dorrance Kennedy

African American Images
Chicago, Illinois

First Edition, First Printing

Copyright by Dr. Dorrance Kennedy

Published by African American Images

Front cover by Nur Design Co.

Printed in the United States

ISBN 9780910030618

This book is dedicated to my late father, Dr. Andrew B. Kennedy

My brother, Drew Kennedy

My son, Elijah Kennedy

And Black men everywhere!!!

CONTENTS

INTRODUCTION

To my Brothers and those who love them:

Too often, Black men try to make it on their own. We do not keep in touch with one another. This reality is very unfortunate. Because Black men have been perceived as a threat to American society. Unwanted and unloved. Despised and disrespected. Feared and hated. And yet envied and imitated. Ironically the spirit and style of Black men has touched the world. Remember Barack Obama, Michael Jordan, Muhammad Ali, Nelson Mandela, and the list goes on and on.

Wisdom from My Father's Porch is inspired by conversations I had with my father before he passed away from cancer. Additionally, it is the result of my experiences raising my own son and my career as a social worker. It is also influenced by personal losses I have experienced by the recent deaths of several of my Black male friends and colleagues. There is an obvious need for Black men to support one another and mentor the next generation. This book is addressed to Black teenagers and young men, parents, educators, and all who interact with young brothers.

CHAPTER 1

SPIRITUALITY

Judgment and Mercy

One of my favorite sayings is that we often want judgment for others and mercy for ourselves. Many of us are critical of other people. We do not believe in giving folks the benefit of the doubt. But we want people to be sympathetic to us and our circumstances. We especially desire judgment when it involves people they do not like. We say, "Remember God doesn't like like ugly." Every dog has its day.

Sympathy is not enough, empathy is needed. Empathy is putting ourselves in other people's shoes. Empathy is a quality that is so desperately missing in our world today. We often pass negative judgment without knowing all the facts. Have you ever been given a second chance? I believe we all have. Have you ever been late to work? Have you ever said something that you later regretted? We have all benefitted from mercy. But when judgment is necessary the punishment should fit the crime.

I want you to consider the case of George Floyd. On Memorial Day 2020, he allegedly paid for merchandise at a store with a fake $20 bill.[1] The question is did he know the bill was fake? It is easy to receive a bogus bill without knowing it. If he knew that the bill was fake, did it justify him losing his life in such a brutal way? Why was he treated like a violent criminal? His life was so violently and callously taken away. We should give people the benefit of the doubt and not be so quick to believe the worst about others.

Have a Relationship with God

As Black folk, it has been invigorating to struggle for freedom and against injustice. However, racism is not the only enemy that we have. We must all struggle against our lower selves. It is good to avoid holding on to grudges, bitterness, and jealousy. Self-destructive habits will not speed up the day of freedom. Our true character is revealed in times of solitude and struggle.

We should not struggle for justice in this world without being certain about our destiny in the world to come. Spiritual freedom is as paramount as liberation from political and economic oppression.

Activists must fortify themselves with spiritual practices such as prayer, fasting, meditation, and worship. Like Stokely Carmichael and Huey Newton, today's activists can burn out too soon. Remember that although Huey P. Newton co-founded the Black Panthers, he later became entangled in substance abuse.[2] Stokely Carmichael (Kwame Ture) ignited the Black Power Movement and Pan-Africanism, yet he died young from the ravages of prostate cancer.[3] We must engage in spiritual self-care. And let us not forget about the importance of the Black church, our most independent institution. The church has been a refuge in a hostile world. Many struggles for freedom have emanated from it.

Prayer

One of the most powerful things we can do in the world is to pray. Prayer is simply talking to God about our needs, concerns, wants, desires. Prayer is also about thanking God for His protection, peace, and provision. Prayer is about telling God how great He is. Prayer is necessary when we are troubled and worried. Prayer is necessary when we are searching for direction. In the words of Stevie Wonder, just have a talk with God. The ACTS model of prayer is very useful. Our prayers should consist of adoration, confession, thanksgiving, and supplication.[4] Adoration is when we honor God for who He is. Our prayers should consist of Confession. We should admit to God the things we have done wrong. Our prayers should consist of Thanksgiving. Thanksgiving is when we tell GOD what we're grateful for. Our prayers should consist of Supplication. Supplication consists of asking God for what we need. Our prayers should not just be about ourselves. Our prayers should also involve sitting still and listening to what God wants to reveal to us.

We Must All Give an Account

Today there are more people who deny the existence of God or believe that one cannot prove or disprove whether God exists. But most people on the planet accept the possibility of a higher spiritual power. The world is simply too complex to rule out the existence of God. Look at your fingerprints. Consider all the plants and trees, oceans and mountains. The sun, moon, and the stars.

Consider the complexity of the human body. Kidneys, lungs, heart, etc. I believe there is a God. There is a great moral law that governs the universe. Alicia Keys called it karma. What comes around, goes around. In other words, you will reap what you sow. Be careful how you treat others, especially the less fortunate. God will hold us accountable for all we do and say. And for all the resources we have been given. The Day of Judgment is coming soon.

CHAPTER 2

FAMILY

Respect Your Elders

As we struggle, we must not forget the bridges that brought us over. The Black freedom struggle consists of five different phases. Jesse Jackson has spoken about the stages of our struggle. The first phase was the struggle to end slavery spearheaded by Frederick Douglass. The second phase was the struggle to end segregation led by Dr. Martin Luther King Jr. The third phase has been the struggle for political representation embodied by the election of President Barack Obama. The fourth and current struggle is for the end of police brutality and mass incarceration. The fifth and final phase that we must engage in is the struggle for economic justice. [1]

In this era of Black Lives Matter, we have become very critical of legacy organizations such as the NAACP and the Urban League. However, these organizations advocated for us in some of our most challenging days. Let us not forget from where we have come from. In the 1980s, Jesse Jackson challenged the rules of winner takes all primaries in his presidential campaigns. He argued that delegates should be awarded in a more proportional way.[2] Without these changes, Obama would have never been elected president of the United States. Yet in Ferguson, Missouri, Jesse Jackson was told by local activists to go home and get out of town.[3]

Thirty years ago, Al Sharpton marched and protested against police brutality and racial violence in New York City.[3] Remember the cases of Michael Griffith, Yusef Hawkins, Sean Bell, the Central Park Five, Amadou Diallo, and Abner Louima.[4] Sadly, tensions have developed between Sharpton and younger activists.

Black Lives Matter is not the first organization to protest police brutality. The Black Panthers began addressing this issue in the mid-sixties. Past generations of activists organized and mobilized without Facebook, Twitter, and cell phones. The youth can benefit from the knowledge and experience of the elders.

Take Care of Moms

You can tell a lot about a man by the way he treats his mother. Our mothers are our first teachers. Most mothers would give anything for their children. Many mothers sacrifice and deny themselves so that their children can have what they need. Many mothers have worked overtime at multiple jobs and caught the early bus to work. They have gone for years without buying a new dress. If these things are true, how should we respond?

Don't forget about your mom when you start dating. Your girlfriend may be fine, but your mother still raised you. Don't forget about your mom when you get married. Your wife comes first. But your momma still raised you. Don't forget about your mom when you're on your own. Don't be too busy to call, send her a card, or go visit her. One day she will get older and her health will fail. Don't abandon her in her time of need. Even Jesus made sure His mother was taken care of, as He was dying on the cross. We should not do any less than that.

Remember Your Pops

I am convinced that Black fathers are often underappreciated. There are countless stories of men who neglect their children and avoid taking care of their responsibilities. But I know several men who are quietly doing their best to be examples of responsibility to their families. I think about men like Richard Williams who coached Venus and Serena into world champion tennis players.[5] I think about Fraser Robinson, the father of Michelle Obama, who raised his family and supported his children in spite of sickness and limited financial resources.[6] Good men too often receive messages from their families that they really don't matter. The message is that their contributions are not a big deal and can be easily replaced. I bear witness today that fathers matter. Fathers have the ability to instill adventure and toughness into their children. There are good fathers and father figures all around. There are coaches, teachers, and mentors. Men are more than just a paycheck or a repair guide. Fathers matter!! We should lift up and honor those men who show up every day without fanfare or recognition. Don't forget the father figures in your life.

Be a Good Husband

The Bible declares that whosoever finds a wife is blessed.[7] A good wife is a blessing to any man. She has great spiritual value in the eyes of God. Your wife craves your attention and affection. She desires your assistance around the house. She wants your listening ear. She wants to know that she comes first in your heart and that she takes priority above all others. Brothers, speak well of your wife. Compliment her in the presence of others. Single her out for special attention. Make her feel special. Learn her love language.[8] Study her well. Know her preferences, hopes, dreams, and fears. Touch her frequently with hugs and kisses. Offer to be of service to make her life more simple. Pour your energy into your wife and she will comfort you in your most challenging hours and brighten your cloudy days.

Don't Be a Player

I want to ask you a question. How many more men will ruin their families, reputations, and careers because they cheated on their partners? Let's be honest. Being a player takes a lot of work and energy. It takes energy to conceal your actions and conversations from the women in your life. Women value openness and honesty and they have a strong sense of intuition when something doesn't seem right.

Many men get careless. It may be a receipt from a restaurant. It may be a text message on your cell phone. It may be lipstick on your shirt. Times have changed. You cannot trust your mistress to keep your secrets. I don't want to see your business on CNN. A moment of pleasure can lead to a lifetime of pain!!! And respect women as the precious individuals that they are. Accusations of sexual harassment and assault can destroy a lifetime of positive deeds. The day of reckoning has come in regard to this type of behavior. Just ask Bill Cosby.

Take Care of Your Children

No one should ever underestimate the impact of a father on his children. The world constantly emphasizes the importance of mothers, but fathers have so much to give. Far too many young men get involved in gangs, drugs, and criminal activities because they have pledged allegiance to a destructive philosophy of manhood. Far too many young women act out sexually or are attracted to negative partners because they are looking for love that they never received from their fathers.[9]

Fathers are able to provide valuable information about being streetwise, mechanical skills, athletics, toughness, and courage. Fathers must often fight for recognition. I have sat in school conferences with my wife at my children's school and sat at the table, being ignored by the teacher. I had to interject myself into the conversation. Black fathers are much more involved than they are given credit for. And please, brothers. Allow your children to grow up in peace. Provide an environment that is safe from abuse. Help them maintain their innocence while they are young. Create childhood experiences that they will cherish for a lifetime.

CHAPTER 3

CULTURE

Cherish Your History

A couple of years ago, I took a family trip to Washington, DC and visited the house of Dr. Carter G. Woodson, the Father of Black History. I could not wait to enter the property to witness greatness. This historical landmark was in disrepair. It has since been rehabbed by the government. With all the wealth that exists in the African American community, why is it necessary for others to refurbish and maintain our institutions? Why do we not cherish our own institutions whether it be the Audubon Ballroom or the Lorraine Motel? We must have enough pride and self-reliance to not allow our history to fall into disrepair.

During the same summer, I visited Virginia where the first Africans arrived as slaves in the year of 1619. At the visitor center, I asked where the marker that highlighted this historical event was. The employees of the center did not know anything about a sign. I was blown away at this display of apathy and ignorance. After much walking, I found a very modest sign. This sign represented the beginning of our great *Mafaa* (a Swahili word meaning African Holocaust).

There is power in our history. We must take a pilgrimage. I have visited the home of Frederick Douglass. I have walked across Selma's Edmund Pettus Bridge, I have stood in the pulpit of Atlanta's Ebenezer Baptist Church. I have traveled to New York City's Audubon Ballroom, where Malcolm last spoke. Many graduates of HBCUs never give back to their alma maters. There is a movement to close or merge these colleges. Many have never given to the Urban League or NAACP. Remember the bridges that brought us over.

Understand How We Became Slaves

In order for us to be effective activists, we must understand how we became slaves. Scholars like Chancellor Williams and

John Henrik Clarke have thoroughly documented how this process took place. Slavery occurred for three reasons: naiveté, lack of unity, and greed for money.[1] First, we were naïve and treated Europeans as guests when they initially came to the shores of Africa.[2] Europeans started exploring Africa's coasts in the late 1400s. The slave trade did not dramatically increase until the late 1600s and early 1700s.

Supposedly, Europeans came to trade goods such as gold and to spread the Gospel as Christian missionaries. Africans showed them hospitality and welcomed their presence and advice. They did not understand that the Europeans had a long-term strategy to rule and conquer. African people also demonstrated a lack of unity. Their loyalty was based on their particular tribe. They did not see themselves as one African people. Additionally, some African leaders willingly sold their own people in pursuit of money, guns, and power. But the majority of African people heroically resisted in the face of superior European military force.

After the slave trade ended, Europeans indulged in a scramble for Africa and implemented a program of colonialism. For example, King Leopold of Belgium is responsible for the death of over 10 million people in the Congo.[3] The suffering of African people has continued for the last 500 years. And yet some of us are still naïve about the ideology of white supremacy. We still are divided by tribe and have a lack of unity. Light skin vs. dark skin. Male vs. female. Elderly vs. young. And some of our people are willing to sell out their people for money.

Unity

It has been said that Black people are like crabs in a barrel. We will sell each other out in order to advance. We will fight each other to the death. The spirit of Willie Lynch is still alive amongst us. We are dreadfully divided by skin color, Greek organization, church denomination, gang affiliation.[4] Why can't we get together? Is it because we came as slaves mixed together by different tribes?

There was a time in which Blacks were more on one accord. We were united in our desire to be free from slavery. There was a time in which Blacks were united in their desire to get out of segregation. We were focused on one big issue. Today we are concerned about many issues—police brutality, poor schools, HBCUs, HIV, mass incarceration, drugs, etc. But in order to move forward, we must once again focus on a major issue that will advance our progress as a people.

It is obvious to me that we need a common code of ethics, a common set of values. Maulana Karenga proposed the NGU-

ZO SABA—unity, self-determination, collective responsibility, cooperative economics, faith, creativity, purpose.[5] In the words of Marcus Garvey, **ONE GOD, ONE AIM, ONE DESTINY!!!**[6]

CHAPTER 4

TROUBLE

Know How to Handle the Police

It is quite evident that being a police officer is a very difficult job. But it is also obvious that there are too many bad cops on our streets and an overall lack of accountability for law enforcement. It is very difficult to indict and convict an officer. We must be wise in our interactions with police. Our immediate goal should be to make it back home alive. It is not a good idea to run from the police, get in an argument, or make any sudden moves. We should be polite and respectful. Keep your hands visible at all times. But even with all these precautions, we are still at risk. It is obvious that we cannot good behavior our way out of the current predicament.

Remember Charles Kinsey, a Black male social worker in Florida, was shot while attempting to keep his autistic client safe.[1] Mr. Kinsey was lying down on the ground with his hands up. Police maintained that Mr. Kinsey was shot by mistake. But after the shooting he was handcuffed on the hot concrete for half an hour. What else could Mr. Kinsey have done to show that he was not a threat? Police need more training. This training should consist of diversity training, cultural sensitivity, psychological testing, and community policing. I believe some police shootings are motivated by an unreasonable fear of people of color.

We must know our rights. We do not have to consent to unreasonable searches. We have the right to remain silent and the right to an attorney. We must demand body cameras, special prosecutors, civilian review boards, and a database of police force against civilians.[2]

Falsely Accused

I have a word of wisdom for you. If you keep on living, you will be accused of something. People may spread rumors and false information about you. Dr. Martin Luther King was once considered a Communist.[3] Nelson Mandela was once considered a terrorist.[4] President Barack Obama has been called a liar, socialist, and a Muslim.[5] Our challenge is to live so that no one will believe them. Too often as Black people, we are guilty until proven innocent. It can take years and lots of effort to redeem your reputation. But there is nothing sweeter than vindication. There is nothing more valuable than a good name.

One day while I was living in New Orleans, I received a letter from the city that I had been convicted of a felony and had lost my right to vote. Obviously, I was very concerned and considered going downtown to the police station to inquire about the situation. I was advised by my lawyer not to go. I could have been arrested on the spot. Two weeks later, the city issued another letter saying that it was a computer glitch. What if I had been stopped by the police for a traffic violation before I received that letter? I would have been heading to the penitentiary. We should remember that not everyone who is in prison is guilty.

It's Not Always Fatal

I remember that one day over ten years ago, I experienced some health problems and I became concerned that it might be terminal. I received an MRI and began to receive mailings from the cancer center. All kinds of emotions went through my mind. I began to think about my wife and young children. I began to think about all my unrealized dreams. To be blunt, I said to myself, I am too young to die.

But I learned, it is not good to accept a death sentence before God says so. Every time you receive a bad report from the doctor, it does not mean that it is time to prepare for your funeral. We have all experienced dismal days when it seems that all hope is gone. But I would encourage you to hold on to your dreams. In essence, it's not over until it's over. I am pleased to report that I am in good health. I am blessed to be alive and in my right mind!!!

I remember watching the NBA Finals a few years ago. The Miami Heat played against the San Antonio Spurs. San Antonio was leading and it looked like it was over for the Heat. The officials put yellow tape around the court and they rolled the champagne into the Spurs' locker room. But somehow, Ray Allen hit a three-point shot from the corner and the Heat made a comeback and won the title.[6] People are often ready to throw you away. But it's not over 'til it's over.

Rejection

It is amazing to consider that Michael Jordan, the greatest basketball player of all time was cut from the high school varsity team as a sophomore.[7] Jordan was so hurt that he cried and wanted his team to lose. Jordan's pain led him to work on his basketball game with a single-minded intensity and determination. Michael Jordan was later taunted and insulted by several high school All-Americans at various camps for his relatively modest high school career. Jordan's legendary competitiveness was driven by his experiences of rejection.

Rejection can give us something to prove. It can give us the eye of the tiger. We can decide to become so excellent that we become irreplaceable. We can turn our pain into power. Be so good that no one will ever be able to say that you are not qualified. Use rejection as your motivation to excel.

Controversy

Sometimes criticism cannot be avoided. You can try to live a righteous life and conduct yourself in an upright manner. But you will be criticized. It is an inevitable part of life. There are times when criticism is justified. We all make mistakes and have defects in our character that need to be corrected. We should strive to use criticism in ways that will make us better, sharper, more self-aware, and humble.

However, sometimes criticism is hurtful, negative, and designed to destroy. Criticism can be both constructive and destructive. Let's be clear!! Leaders will be criticized. Leaders cannot please all the people, all the time. Some people will think the leader is moving too fast, others will feel that the movement is too slow. The leader is too tough or too easygoing. Taking a stand on a tough issue can earn you great opposition. The best course of action is to humbly decide what's right, make a decision, and stand up firmly on principle.

CHAPTER 5

TIME

The Clock Is Ticking

Dr. Martin Luther King Jr. said that procrastination is the thief of time. He spoke about "the fierce urgency of now."[1] We should stop living like we have a thousand years to live. Some of us move so slowly. We always talk about what we are going to do but don't always get around to it. We must always remember that we have a limited amount of time to make our impact.

Now is the time to go back to college

Now is the time to start that business

Now is the time to forgive a friend

Now is the time to lose that weight

Now is the time to redeem our communities

You will not always be young. You may be 18 or 21 or 25 now. But you will soon be 45 and middle-aged. You will soon be 60 and looking forward to retirement. Your children will soon be grown and gone. Where did all the time go? The wealthiest place in the world is the cemetery because no one there has any bills to pay. And so many people die with their dreams unfulfilled. We must be very intentional about our time and how we spend our energy. If we are not intentional, we will spend eternity asking ourselves what happened.

What Is Your Plan?

There is power in the details. As an aspiring leader, you must be able to articulate a plan of action. Your plan must be realistic and reasonable.

Are you going to college?

What will you major in?

What part of the country will you live in?

Do you plan to get married?

How much will you save for retirement?

What is your dream job?

How many children will you have?

Where will you be in the next five–ten years?

How will you reduce your debt?

How will you save money?

A plan must have timelines and deadlines. You must have a plan.

Tomorrow is not Promised

One February morning, at the beginning of Black History Month, I received a phone call. A friend of mine named Demetrius who lived in St. Louis had been murdered. It came as a shock. I had just visited St. Louis a couple of weeks before and saw him at our pastor's retirement banquet. I went over and embraced him and told him that he and his wife made a great looking couple. We took pictures together and then I got the phone call that he was DEAD. GONE. NEVER TO RETURN. How could this have happened??? What did he do wrong??? He simply went on a date night with his wife and three other couples. Dinner and then bowling. A couple of young guys began arguing at the bowling alley. Someone called the police. The fight was over by the time the cops arrived. One of the guys went to the parking lot and got his gun. He approached my friend's car and shot while his wife sat next to him. Was it a case of mistaken identity?? Or just evil?? Or just foolishness?? In a few hours he was gone. Please say it's not so. 45 years old. Married for 20 years, father of two children, an ordained minister. A Black man doing all the right things. Shot dead by another Black man. What a wake-up call!! I have a photo of me and Demetrius up in my office as a constant reminder. Follow through on the things that are in your heart. Get started today because LIFE IS SHORT and TOMORROW IS NOT PROMISED.

CHAPTER 6

CHARACTER

You're Being Watched

No matter where you go, somebody is watching you. With the prevalence of technology, you must assume that there's a camera everywhere and that your words and actions are being recorded. We live in a world where there is an illusion of privacy. People surf the internet not aware that they are leaving a digital footprint that can be traced.

Employers are examining job applicants' Facebook pages and credit scores to determine if they are suitable for the job. True character has been defined as who you are when nobody is watching. Before deciding to undertake an action, consider if it will pass the smell test. Will it stink once it comes to the light of day? If you see a friend or colleague get caught doing wrong and you are involved in a similar activity, it should be a warning sign for us to stop or adjust our behavior. Accept the reality that there are no real secrets in the world.

Stand on Your Own

I love the famous song by Billie Holiday, "God Bless the Child That's Got His Own". It sums up the reality of our lives. We are often fooled by the promise of human companionship. It may be true that our lives are made easier by our family and friends. But we are required to bear our own burden. It is true that no individual can help you more than you help yourself. Black people must spend more time building up the institutions of their community as they do in protesting conditions of injustice. Marcus Garvey said that our tendency to expect others to help us without making the effort to do for ourselves has created strong prejudice against us.[1] We cannot beg and fight at the same time.

Integrity

Tell the truth and shame the devil

We lie about all kinds of things

We lie about how old we are

We lie about how much money we make

We lie about how tall we are

We lie about how much we weigh

Oftentimes, the stories we tell are driven by pride. We want to make ourselves look better than what we are. It is our desire to impress other people and that leads us to shade the truth. If we are going to be leaders and people of influence, we must have the capacity to tell the truth. There are cameras and cell phones everywhere. We are always being watched. There is nothing secret. Our illusion of privacy leads us to take chances with the truth. Nobody trusts a liar and liars can't lead.

Don't Give Up Too Soon

I have wanted to quit so many times. I wanted to drop out of school, but I couldn't. I wanted to stop being responsible, but I couldn't. Times may get tough, but if you can hang in there, you just might catch your second wind and learn some valuable life lessons. You may learn to be more patient and learn the value of persisting and persevering against the odds. We must not spend our time cussing and fussing. One time, I traveled out of town for a conference. On the way back home, I left my suit bag on the plane and my cell phone in the bathroom. By the time I was able to retrieve these items, the gate to my connecting flight had changed. I ran through the terminal and made it there in the nick of time. Nobody knew everything I went through to make it there. Regardless of our struggles, we must show up on time. I have learned that through the prayers of many and by the grace of God, we can win. I have learned many lessons about patience and perseverance. We must grow and mature and refuse to quit. We must run on and see what the end is going to be.

Know When to Leave

It is not good to overstay your welcome. We have all been in situations where we become restless. Sometimes we feel these emotions because it is time for us to go. Whenever you begin to dread going to work or you feel yourself just going through the motions. Maybe it's time. Whenever you feel your motivation lagging and you struggle to live up to your own standards of performance maybe it's time to go.

Have you hit the ceiling where you are? Have you maximized your potential? Have you made your contribution? Have you done all you can do in the situation you're in? At times, we must seek new challenges and new opportunities to develop ourselves. Don't become complacent and lose your edge. A new position or a different location may provide unforeseen opportunities. God can move anywhere. But there are times when your location can affect your destiny. It's not easy to get into show business when you live in Idaho. Sometimes, you must go to where the action is.

Be Humble

I have always loved sports. One of my childhood heroes was Dr. J, Julius Erving of the Philadelphia 76ers. A lot of people forget that Dr. J was Michael Jordan before there was a Jordan. Perhaps Jordan had a more well-rounded game and won more championships but Dr. J brought a new level of excitement, artistry, and class to the game that was unprecedented.

One thing I loved about the Doctor is that he would defy gravity and demonstrate unbelievable skill and then jog down the court as if nothing happened. I was deeply impressed by his example. His style is a lesson for all of us. Nothing will gain you more respect than to be a performer of extraordinary skill and to be humble in your demeanor.

It is best to under-promise and over-deliver. Be modest about yourself and your achievements. Allow people to be pleasantly surprised and astounded by your abilities. Too many people walk around pretending that they are more than who they really are. Don't be one of them. Let your work speak for you. It's a joy to shock people with your biography.

CHAPTER 7

MENTALITY

Believe in Yourself

I have always been a little shy. I always felt different from my peers. I was shorter than all my friends. I was a Black male in a predominately white environment. I was among people who demonstrated an abundance of self-confidence. But I have learned through failure and experience that self-confidence is essential to success. You must believe in yourself if you expect others to believe in you. The reality is that self-confidence is necessary to leadership.

Today, my self-confidence is based on not only my abilities or achievements but in my identity as a believer. I am able to succeed because I am empowered by a force greater than myself. Everybody has faults and shortcomings. Everyone is trying to compensate in some way. People hide their insecurities; they are not always as sure as they seem to be. You are just as good as anybody else. Sometimes it is necessary to take action while you are afraid.

Enthusiasm

Ralph Waldo Emerson once said, "Nothing great was ever achieved without enthusiasm."[1] If we want to be successful, we must have passion. Why does it seem that people who do wrong have an abundance of energy and personality? They are charismatic, full of life and vigor. But the good people??? People like you and I who go to work every day. Pay their taxes. Raise their children. Vote. Go to church. Too often, these folks are so BORING!!!

We must do the right thing and make it appear exciting. We must make going to school, getting married, saving money, maintaining our families, and standing up for our communities seem exciting again. It is exciting to earn your way. It is exciting to do the right thing so that you can walk through the world proud and unafraid. Get fired up and inspire somebody to be better.

Be Diverse, Well-Rounded

It is so important to be diverse in various fields of endeavor. All of us need to concentrate on developing our talents and gifts to produce multiple streams of income. It is dangerous to solely rely on a 9–5 job. We must analyze ourselves. What talents do you have that you can turn into a legitimate business?

I have been inspired by the example of James Weldon Johnson who achieved in so many ways. Raised in Jacksonville, Florida, he became a principal and was the first Black man to be admitted to the bar in Duval County, Florida. He wrote the Negro National Anthem, "Lift Every Voice and Sing." He was a United States diplomat to Venezuela and Nicaragua. He was an author, poet, college professor, and Executive Secretary of the NAACP.[2] Or consider Gordon Parks who was a well renowned photographer, pianist, semipro basketball player. He wrote nearly a dozen books, including *The Learning Tree*, and directed movies.[3] Be excellent in multiple ways.

Control Your Anger, Apologize

The Good Book says we should be quick to hear, slow to speak, slow to wrath. It also states that the anger of man cannot achieve the righteousness of God.[4] I am normally a very calm, even-tempered person. But I am ashamed to admit that a few times I have lost my cool. I can remember attending my son's basketball game a couple of years ago. I felt the other team was playing unfairly and I began to point it out to the referee. The next thing you know, the opposing coach's team walked off the court and the referee got in my face. We began arguing. I know I could have handled it in a better way. My children were watching me as well as one of my former coworkers. I regretted my actions.

Simple conversations can quickly get out of control. We must develop the skills to de-escalate situations, seek common ground, interject humor, and stay calm. A wise man once said that the challenge is to improve our argument and not raise our voices. When we become angry, we may do and say things that we will regret for a lifetime. We must learn to deal with anger in a constructive way. Holding on to anger can affect our health and our relationships. Don't let the sun go down on your wrath. Sometimes it is wise to stay cool and apologize, even when we feel that we are right.

Learn the Lesson

Have you ever found yourself confronted with the same issue over and over again? It may be a sign that we have not learned the lesson. What is life saying to you right now? What is the message from the universe? Are you consistently attracting toxic people into your life? Do you find yourself having challenges because you are procrastinating, spending money carelessly, neglecting your health, or trusting the wrong folks???

We have to be wise enough to recognize patterns in our lives. If we see the pattern, we can reverse course and avoid relapsing back into the same behavior. But if we don't recognize the pattern, history ends up repeating itself. Even if we change our surroundings and meet new people, we end up having the same experiences in new places.

The same wisdom applies to individuals and nations. After the end of slavery, segregation began because we did not learn the lesson. After the beating of Rodney King (1991), there were the murders of Trayvon Martin (2012) and Eric Garner (2014) because we did not learn the lesson. The lesson will keep coming at you until you realize what's happening and learn the lesson. School is in session, LEARN THE LESSON.

Be Patient

Things don't always happen when we would like. Many times there is a reason for the delay. Maybe we are not ready for the things that we want. Maybe the thing that we desire will be too much for us or maybe certain situations will not utilize our gifts and talents in the best way. I have been impatient about many things in my life. I remember many times where I desired to be in a place other than where I was. When I was in junior high, I couldn't wait until high school. When I was in high school, I couldn't wait for college. When I was in college, I couldn't wait to graduate. I am middle-aged now and I wish that I could slow the years down.

There is value in every stage of life. We must master one stage before we are allowed to proceed to the next level. Wherever you are today, keep working and believing that your change will come. There is a plan for our lives that we don't always fully understand. Work hard, be patient, your time will come.

Don't Let Dreams Die

The word *veto* means the official power or right to refuse to allow something to be done. The president or governor has the power to veto legislation. The power to stop progress. The power to overrule a decision. Sometimes in life, people will try to veto your dreams. They will tell you that your dreams are unrealistic or unreasonable. They say your plans will never work. Don't allow anyone to veto your destiny. Don't give anyone the power to tell you what can't happen. During a crime scene, people will put yellow tape around the perimeter. Some folks want to put a yellow tape around your life, your plans, your hopes, your ambitions. Don't allow them to do it.

Maybe only you can see the vision of the future. I read a story one day about Harriet Tubman. She was the leader of the Underground Railroad. She was a slave who had a dream of freedom. She decided to make her escape and tried to convince her husband to go with her. He laughed at her and threatened to turn her in. She escaped and later returned to convince him again. However, he refused to leave the plantation. If she had listened to him, she would have died on the plantation.[5] Don't let your dreams die. Don't allow folks with no vision to veto your destiny.

Don't Miss the Layup

I played basketball in junior high school. I was a pretty good player. I played point guard and I was short and quick. I was able to move through the opposing team's defense and get to the open court. There was only one problem. I would dribble down the court all by myself and then miss the layup!! This happened over and over. I did not understand it. I did all that work to get open and then I would miss the opportunity to score. Some people in life do the same thing. After you have worked hard, you must have the skills to close the deal and put the ball in the basket. Don't choke when opportunity stares you in the face.

Don't Be a Bully

I have always had a heart for the underdog. As I was growing up, I saw kids who were smaller, weaker, or different being picked on. Being a bully is never cool. We should use our strength to protect and encourage others. We must learn to respect everyone we come in contact with. You can tell a great deal about a person by the way that they handle authority. How do you use your authority? Do you use your position to intimidate, control, or dominate others? Do you want others around you to bow down and kiss your ring? Do you take advantage of those who are smaller, weaker, younger, or in some way more vulnerable than you?

You will often discover that bullies are not as tough as they appear to be. They are often cowards. It is interesting to consider that the Ku Klux Klan covered their faces, often attacked at night, and always traveled in groups. Bullies often need a weapon or a crowd of people to confront you. They will catch you by surprise. But a real person of courage will take a stand in broad daylight. A person of courage is willing to stand alone against popular opinion for what is right.

CHAPTER 8

KNOWLEDGE

Read

Let me be clear, I love books and I always have. I am a biblio-
phile, a lover and collector of books. I put up eighteen shelves
in my garage and still cannot accommodate them all. I have so
many that I need to rent a storage space to hold them all. Why
do I read so much? Because I love to seek knowledge. There is
a power in knowing about a wide variety of topics. Reading can
transport you out of your environment. You can learn from the
experiences of world-class leaders and travelers. You can gain
wisdom from people who have achieved great things.

In order to be a great leader or activist, we must learn from the experiences of those who have gone before us. Stokely Carmichael once said that revolutions must be based on historical analysis.[1] We must read and understand Frederick Douglass, Booker T. Washington, Harriet Tubman, Sojourner Truth, Ida B. Wells, A. Philip Randolph, etc., in order to navigate current and future struggles. We must grapple with classic texts such as *Up from Slavery, The Souls of Black Folk, The Mis-Education of the Negro, The Autobiography of Malcolm X, The New Jim Crow.* Marcus Garvey owned 18,000 books.[2] The greatest leaders of our time have been voracious readers. It has often been said that readers are leaders.

Go to College

I have always enjoyed being on the college campus. It is exciting to be in an environment where people are discussing and debating ideas. College campuses have always been places where future leaders are developed. Martin Luther King was transformed at Morehouse College. W. E. B. Du Bois was made new at Fisk. Jesse Jackson was changed at North Carolina A&T.

At college, we meet classmates who may become professional colleagues and even lifelong friends. Today's economy requires more education to compete. A bachelor's degree is the same as yesterday's high school diploma. Pursue all the education you can. Knowledge is truly power. The educational process teaches critical thinking skills, builds character, and produces patience.

Travel

A couple of years ago, I had the opportunity to travel abroad for the first time. I went to the west coast of Africa and visited the nation of Ghana. While I was there, I visited the famous slave castles at Elmina and stood at the Door of No Return. I traveled to the capital city of Accra and toured many parts of the nation. There were parts of the country that were very well-developed and other areas that were seriously underdeveloped.

I witnessed mounds of trash on the street and chickens and goats walking around. I had to drink bottled water and take malaria medication. I encountered young men who eagerly sold products on the street. I was inspired by their zeal and entrepreneurial spirit. I struggled to shave my face with my electric clippers. I heard about practices of sexual slavery on the outskirts of the country. Before I left the U.S., I had to obtain a passport and visa and many immunization shots. It was very educational. It made me appreciate America and all we have compared to others around the globe. Travel will make you aware of issues you may have never considered.

CHAPTER 9

RELATIONSHIPS

Make a Deposit, Invest in People

In the world in which we live, we often use people and love things. However, we should love people and use things. We must take the time to invest in people. How do we invest? Every human being on the planet needs encouragement, especially those who are hurting or less fortunate than ourselves. We must encourage people to not give up hope. We can invest by giving somebody a second chance who has made a mistake. There are many people in our community who have criminal records and need another opportunity for jobs, housing, etc.

We can invest in people by teaching them a skill or helping them to develop their gifts, talents, or abilities. We all know people who only call us when they need something. It is much better to take the time to nurture and build relationships so that when we need assistance, we have already built up a strong supply of goodwill.

Call People First, Call People Back

I have a lot of friends that I never hear from unless I call them. It's amazing that we are not more vigilant about maintaining and nurturing our relationships. Relationships take much time, energy, patience, and communication. We allow weeks and months to go by without talking. We will continue to remain oppressed as long as we stay disconnected. Too many people maintain that they are too busy to call. However, we should never be too busy to pick up the phone.

I have a creative idea for "busy" people. You can send a text message or call and leave a voice mail at a time when they are unlikely to answer their phone. The truth is that not calling people back is rude and disrespectful. We should strive to call people back within two days. Are we really that busy? Some parents don't call their own children and yet get mad when there is no communication. We should not allow weeks and months to go by. Relationships require time and attention. It is not good when one person is doing all of the calling and reaching out. Reciprocity should be a watchword of our relationships. Good relationships require give-and-take.

Listen More Than You Talk

It has been said that God gave us two ears and only one mouth for a reason. So the question is, why do we talk so much?? I am a relatively quiet person. After a certain amount of time, I get tired of hearing my own voice. But there are some people in the world who seem to be mesmerized by the sound of their own voices. The truth is that the more you talk, the greater chance you are going to say something inappropriate, unkind, or unnecessary.

I make it a rule to not speak about subjects that I am not well versed about. It is amazing to hear people give their opinions about things that they are ignorant about and speak with total confidence. Also, we all have met people who are so engaged in their own conversation that they are totally blind to nonverbal communication. If somebody is looking at their watch, rolling their eyes, or moving away from you, it may be a sign to BE QUIET!!!.

Keep Confidences

All of us need somebody to talk to. All of us have to decide who to trust. When somebody confides in you it is an awesome responsibility to live up to that expectation. Have you ever had the experience of sharing something very personal with somebody and later they shared that sensitive information with another person? Have you ever had the experience of sharing something with someone and they throw it back in your face during a later conversation? How did that make you feel?

We should strive to be a guardian of others' vulnerabilities. Once we betray those who have trusted us, don't be surprised if they become much more reserved and distant. The Good Book says that love covers a multitude of sins.[1] We should cover the faults and shortcomings of those we claim to love. How many times has somebody covered you?

Boundaries

We all have relationships in our lives. But all of our relationships are not the same. We have associates, friends, and confidants. Associates are people we know in our social setting. They may be coworkers or neighbors. We do not have deep relationships with them. We may have surface conversations with them. We spend limited time with them. These are hi and bye relationships. We are cordial and pleasant but we rarely share personal things about ourselves with them.

Next we have friends. These are more personal relationships. We may hang out with them and reveal personal things about ourselves to them. We generally like them and can call on them when we need assistance. Lastly, we have confidants. These individuals make up our inner circle. We can be very open and vulnerable with them and they will come to our aid when times are really tough.

It is not wise to get these relationships confused. It is good to avoid dual relationships. Be careful about making an associate into a friend or confidant especially if you are their supervisor. Always remember that business is business. We should maintain boundaries. Sometimes dual relationships can hinder achievement.

Fake Folks

I want to let you know that there are a lot of fake folks in the world. Some people call them fair-weather friends. They will pretend that they have your best interests at heart. Their intentions are not true. Their laughs are not real. They have a double agenda. Watch your back, be careful what you tell them. You are not speaking confidentially. Your words may later be used against you. They may be jealous of you or feel threatened. They win your confidence only to betray your trust. Be careful who you trust.

CHAPTER 10

COMMUNITY

Get Involved

A major problem with Black people is that we are reactionary. Instead of being proactive about our quest for freedom, we often react after some injustice has taken place. In order to obtain freedom, we must forever remain vigilant. Our responses to injustice have become too predictable. We cannot just get involved only when it is popular to do so. We must be active and engaged at all times, even when it is not sexy. We must focus on the boring essentials. Register to vote. Serve on juries. Join organizations. Donate money. Volunteer at your local school.

When I lived in St. Louis, I became involved with grassroots organizations that were working on the issue of police brutality, civilian review boards, and police accountability. These meetings were sparsely attended. Over ten years later, Ferguson, Missouri, exploded because of the murder of Michael Brown. Perhaps more proactive community activism could have prevented this tragedy.

After the murder of Trayvon Martin, there was some discussion of boycotting Tropicana.[1] These actions never materialized. Let's pick an issue to become involved in and make a difference in our corner of the world. Consistent pressure is necessary to make change. The three things that are killing us are ignorance, apathy, and cynicism. Let us study the issues, be concerned about our fellow brothers and sisters and believe that change can happen.

Be a Mentor

In the Black community, we frequently talk about the importance of mentoring. By mentoring, I simply mean guiding, directing, or encouraging someone who is often younger and less experienced than you are. We constantly talk about mentoring but the sad reality is that we do not do a good job of mentoring in a practical sense of the word. Mentors should possess certain qualities and characteristics.

First, there must be a true willingness or desire to mentor and be of service to someone else. Second, there must be availability. The mentor must make himself available. He must set aside time in his schedule to assist, teach, and guide the mentee. Third, there must be security. The mentor must be secure in who they are and the talents they possess. The mentor cannot be threatened by the potential of the mentee. Fourth, there must be transparency. The mentor must be open to share lessons learned and mistakes made. Too many people are too caught up in their own lives to help somebody else.

Volunteer

There's a disturbing trend in society today. Some people will not get involved with anything unless they are getting paid. This "pay to serve" mentality is damaging our society and especially our youth. Many successful and prominent people have gained valuable experience serving as an intern or an apprentice. No dollar amount can be placed on the opportunity to learn from others who can share from their expertise and wealth of knowledge.

Some people have volunteered their way into a job. Some people have volunteered their way into a promotion. You can make yourself valuable at your job by volunteering for extra responsibilities. You can make yourself valuable in the community by volunteering at your local school, agency, or civil rights organization. Community service can lead to college scholarships, professional connections, and employment opportunities. Be of service. VOLUNTEER!!!

Leave a Good Record Behind

Wherever you are try to make a positive contribution. Leave a mark that cannot be erased. You want to leave things better than you found it. If you perform your job with an attitude of integrity and excellence, people will remember you and often welcome you back. When you are known for going above and beyond the call of duty, people will remember you. It is really all about legacy. What do you want to be remembered for? Can you do something today that will affect future generations? Aspire to be a game changer. Impact others by your performance. Place your footprints in the sands of time.

GEORGE WASHINGTON CARVER left a legacy

A. G. GASTON left a legacy

CHARLES DREW left a legacy

LEWIS LATIMER left a legacy

MARTIN LUTHER KING left a legacy

NELSON MANDELA left a legacy

BARACK OBAMA left a legacy

MICHAEL JORDAN left a legacy

What will your legacy be??

CHAPTER 11

APPEARANCE

Stay in Shape

When I was young, I wanted to be bigger and more muscular. My mother used to tell me to be happy with the size I was. I did not listen. I still wanted to be bigger. There was a time when I could eat anything I wanted and not gain weight. Well, those days are over!! My waist size has expanded and there are some pants I can no longer fit into. In fact, everywhere you go there is food. Beware of the holidays!! Beware of vacations!! Beware of lunchtime at work!! Beware of going out to eat. Stay away from certain people's houses. People are always offering food. Temptation is all around, but you must resist!!!

Watch what you eat. Limit red meat, fast foods, salt, and sweets. Eat more raw and living food. Our ability to maintain a healthy weight largely depends on our diet. And remember to exercise. Engage in weight lifting and high intensity training. High blood pressure and hypertension are plaguing the Black community. Strokes are on the rise. Keep sickness away and the hospital at bay. Nelson Mandela spent 27 years in prison and came out a vigorous man because of his rigorous daily exercise routine. In order to be a champion, you must take care of your temple. HEALTH IS TRULY WEALTH.

Dress Well

People will judge you by your appearance. This is an unpleasant but true fact of life. For many years, Black people were subject to many stereotypes. We were considered less intelligent, less patriotic, and more violent. And then there were the myths that we were descended from the apes and that we smelled bad. Experts believed that are brains were smaller. Theologians taught that Black folk did not have souls and could not go to heaven. Dressing well has always been an important part of African American culture. During the days of the Civil Rights

Movement, marchers dressed up in suits and dresses. As they demonstrated for freedom and equality, they knew it was important to look the part.

Always remember. We must look the part. Faith it until you make it. The habit of walking around with no belts on, showing our underwear, and being covered with tattoos may not serve us well in professional settings. We must invest in classic clothes that stand the test of time. It is important to say that dressing well does not require a fortune. LOOK FOR SALES!!! It is good to avoid clothes that represent today's trends but will be considered out of style tomorrow. There are few things more impressive than an African American man who is well educated, well-spoken, and well-dressed. Remember the style of Martin Luther King, Johnnie Cochran, and Nelson Mandela. Clothes still do make the man!!

Status Affects Service

I have learned how important status is in the service that we receive. Too often, people assign low status to others because of race, socioeconomic class, and personal appearance. But the reality is that you never know with whom you are interacting.

I went to dinner at a restaurant with my family a couple of years ago. As I was looking at the menu, I ordered my customary iced tea. As I was sipping my drink, a dead fly entered my straw and hit me on the lips. I was shocked and outraged. I called my waitress over and pointed out the issue. I was amazed at how nonchalant she was. I also spoke with the manager. I reflected on how much our status affects the service we receive. Recently I went to my local bank to cash a check. The teller gave me ten dollars extra without my knowledge. The next day the bank called me and requested that I return the extra money to the bank. I wondered why this multimillion-dollar corporation was contacting me about an error made by their employee. Would a "high status" customer have been treated the same way? We have seen this issue of status in modern times. Trayvon Martin was profiled by George Zimmerman because he was a "low status" African American male who wore a hoodie with perceived criminal tendencies.[1]

CHAPTER 12

MONEY AND CAREER

Be an Entrepreneur

The Honorable Marcus Garvey said that you should never wait on another man's pocketbook.[1] The economy is a very uncertain. Layoffs, downsizing, and government shutdowns are real possibilities. When we are totally dependent on one source of income, we are vulnerable economically. This is the question. Are there skills and gifts within you that can translate into profit? How can you create multiple streams of income? The painful reality is that no one can truly pay you what you are worth. Have you ever had problems or challenges on the job? Have you felt underappreciated and underpaid? Are you tired of the office politics at your place of employment? Has your path to promotion been blocked? Maybe it is a sign that you should branch out on your own.

Have a Trade

As a professor, I can tell you that college is not for everybody. I have met students who simply lack the skills and the seriousness to succeed academically. Some individuals simply don't enjoy the rigor required to think critically, attend class regularly, and study diligently. My college classes are filled with female students and very few men.

Perhaps it is because men are more focused on finding a quicker method to make money. Past generations of men have supported their families by working as plumbers, electricians, carpenters, barbers, etc. Community colleges and vocational training are legitimate options for those who seek training that may directly lead them into gainful employment. I agree wholeheartedly with W. E. B. Du Bois that higher education provides wonderful opportunities for personal and professional growth.[2] I also agree with Booker T. Washington that education must be more practical than philosophical.[3] College is not for everybody but we must all find a way to support ourselves and our families.

Get Out of Debt, Save Money

Millions of people struggle with credit card debt. We are tempted to spend money on things we do not need. Television commercials are designed to make us spend money. We are lured in by great sales to buy things that we really don't need. We are trapped in high interest debt. Being in debt is like having an addiction. American culture encourages dissatisfaction among its people. The consumer mentality demands something newer, bigger, and slicker. We must stay out of environments that tempt us to spend unnecessarily and avoid impulse spending. We can never be free as long as we are drowning in debt. We can never be free when we are living a couple of paychecks away from poverty. Today, unemployment is on the rise because of COVID-19.

There's More Than Dollars

We live in a consumer society. It is wise to find something that you love to do and make a living at it. There are millions of people around the world that are stuck in jobs that they dislike. It is a terrible situation to be forced to go to a job that you hate. The old saying goes, follow your passion and the money will follow. What's your price? Are there ideals and principles that are so precious to you, that you will not compromise? Is anything sacred anymore? I remember in the 1990s, Rosa Parks was living alone in Detroit, her house was broken into by a young African American man named Joseph Skipper. She asked him did he know who she was. He said yes and proceeded to beat her up.[4] Was it worth it? Is anything sacred anymore?

CHAPTER 13

HEALTH AND WELL-BEING

Beware of Guns

I grew up in New Orleans. I lived there for twenty years. In the 1990s, New Orleans was the murder capital of the United States. The nature of conflict has changed. There was a time when young men settled their differences with their fists. But today, we are quick to resolve our conflict with guns. It takes wisdom to de-escalate conflict. The truth is that some men are cowards without their weapons. Some men who are unable to defend themselves with their hands act like warriors because of their weapons. We should think carefully before we act. In some cases, loved ones, children, and innocent bystanders have been killed. What a tragic loss of life. We have lost too many brothers in the streets. Learn self-defense. Take martial arts classes so that you may be able to defend yourself when the time comes.

Jail

To put it bluntly, stay out of jail. Mass incarceration is real. In the 1980s, President Reagan declared the War on Drugs shortly before crack cocaine emerged on the streets of America.[1] People who were nonviolent offenders needing treatment were locked up. Mandatory minimum sentences were used to impose harsh sentences. Major corporations began to invest in private prisons. A person convicted of a felony in the United States suffers from reduced life options. They have been denied the right to vote, the right to live in public housing, access to federal student financial aid, and barred from several types of jobs. Inmates may be physically and sexually abused as well. Criminal justice in America is big business. The focus is on profit and not rehabilitation.

Don't Take Yourself Out

Suicide is on the rise in the Black community. Men often do not share their innermost feelings. Unresolved grief and anger can cause many problems. These issues can affect men from all walks of life. Sometimes bad news comes in bunches and the rain keeps on falling. Bad events fall down like dominoes. When bad things keep on happening, we need good coping skills. Prayer, exercise, counseling, and meditation come to mind. However, when our normal coping mechanisms don't work, we can easily find ourselves in a crisis. Significant losses in our careers, health, finances, or personal lives can cause pain. Grief has many stages: denial, anger, bargaining, depression, and finally acceptance.[2] The foundations of our world have been shaken because of COVID-19. We all need support and we must be gentle with ourselves. Don't be afraid to ask for support. Don't solve a temporary situation with a final solution.

Go See the Doctor and a Counselor

This is a message to Black men everywhere. Take care of your health. We must commit to regular medical checkups. It is important to know what your vitals are. Stress is killing us. Blood pressure, cholesterol, glucose level. Prostate cancer, sickle cell anemia. It is important to visit our primary care doctor as well as the dentist and ophthalmologist. Don't forget your mental health. Anxiety and depression can take a heavy toll. Too many brothers are dying young. Andre Harrell, Prince, Michael Jackson. Gone too soon. We have lost too many brothers. Black man, you have infinite value in the eyes of God. You are the original man of the earth. Value yourself, love yourself, and take care of yourself. We must support each other and guide the next generation. Let us unite, mobilize, and change the world.

ENDNOTES

Chapter 1: Spirituality

Matt Furber, Audra Burch, and Frances Robles, "What Happened in the Chaotic Moments before George Floyd Died," *The New York Times*, May 29, 2020. https://www.nytimes.com/2020/05/29/us/derek-chauvin-george-floyd-worked-together.html

David Hilliard, *Huey: Spirit of the Panther* (New York: Thunder's Mouth Press, 2006).

Peniel Joseph, *Stokely: A Life* (New York: Civitas Books, 2016).

Kathryn Shirey, "How to Pray with the ACTS Prayer Method," Prayer and Possibilities, December 2, 2018. https://www.prayerandpossibilities.com/acts-a-guide-to-pray-as-jesus-taught/

Chapter 2: Family

1. Jesse Jackson, *The Stages of Struggle* [Video]. YouTube. April 18, 2018. https://www.youtube.com/watch?v=HPVIMPRsBkc

2. Ta-Nehisi Coates, "The Tragedy of Jesse Jackson," *The Atlantic*, July 14, 2008. https://www.theatlantic.com/entertainment/archive/2008/07/the-tragedy-of-jesse-jackson/4984

3. Philip Swarts, "Ferguson Protesters Confront Jesse Jackson: 'When You Going to Stop Selling Us Out,'" *Washington Times*, August 23, 2014. https://www.washingtontimes.com/news/2014/aug/23/ferguson-protesters-confront-jesse-jackson-when-yo/

4. Randolph Jacoby, *Civil Rights Leaders: Al Sharpton* (Broomall: Mason Crest, 2019).

5. Wayne D'Orio, *Al Sharpton: Civil Rights* (New York: Chelsea House, 2011).

6. James Buckley, *Who Are Venus and Serena Williams?* (New York: Penguin Random House, 2017).

7. David Mendell, *Obama: From Promise to Power* (New York: Amistad, 2007).

8. Proverbs 18:22, *NIV and KJV Side-by-Side Bible* (Grand Rapids: Zondervan, 2011).

9. Gary Chapman, *The Five Love Languages: The Secret to Love that Lasts* (Chicago: Northfield Publishing, 2015).

10. Jonetta Rose Barras, *Whatever Happened to Daddy's Little Girl?* (New York: Ballantine Publishing Group, 2000).

Chapter 3: Culture

1. Chancellor Williams, *The Destruction of Black Civilization* (Chicago: Third World Press, 1987).

2. John Henrik Clarke, *Christopher Columbus and the Afrikan Holocaust* (Buffalo: EWorld, 1993).

3. Don Nardo, *The European Colonization of Africa* (Greensboro: Morgan Reynolds, 2011).

4. Alvin Morrow, *Breaking the Curse of Willie Lynch* (St. Louis: Rising Sun Publications, 2003).

5. Maulana Karenga, *Introduction to Black Studies* (Los Angeles: University of Sankore Press, 1993).

6. Amy Jacques Garvey, ed., *The Philosophy and Opinions of Marcus Garvey* (Dover: The Majority Press, 1986).

Chapter 4: Trouble

1. Charles Rabin, "Unarmed Black Therapist Shot by Cop Thanks Jury for Finding Officer Negligent," *Miami Herald*, June 20, 2019. https://www.miamiherald.com/news/local/crime/article231749238.html

2. Campaign Zero: We Could End Police Violence in America. https://www.joincampaignzero.org/#vision

3. Richard Severo, "Dr. King and Communism: No Link Ever Produced," *The New York Times*, October 22, 1983. https://www.nytimes.com/1983/10/22/us/dr-king-and-communism-no-link-ever-produced.html

4. Olivia Waxman, "The United States Government Had Nelson Mandela on Terrorist Watch List until 2008. Here's Why," *Time*, July 18, 2018. https://www.time.com/5338569/nelson-mandela-terror-list/

5. Peter Ferrera, "Is President Obama Really a Socialist? Let's Analyze Obamanomics," *Forbes*, December 20, 2012. https://www.forbes.com/sites/peterferrera/2012/12/20/is-president-obama-really-a-socialist-lets-analyze-obamanomics/#2dffe287d008

6. DJ Siddiqi, "Ray Allen Speaks Out on Epic Game-Tying Shot vs. Spurs in 2013 Finals," Clutch Points, April 13, 2020. https://www.clutchpoints.com/heat-news-ray-allen-speaks-out-on-epic-game-tying-shot-in-2013-finals

7. Sean Dolan, *Michael Jordan: Basketball Great* (New York: Chelsea House, 1994).

Chapter 5: Time

1. James Washington, ed., *A Testament of Hope: The Essential Writings and Speeches of Martin Luther King, Jr.* (New York: Harper One, 2003).

Chapter 6: Character

1. Amy Jacques Garvey, ed., *The Philosophy and Opinions of Marcus Garvey* (Dover: The Majority Press, 1986).

Chapter 7: Mentality

1. Ralph Waldo Emerson and Brooks Atkinson, ed., *The Essential Writings of Ralph Waldo Emerson* (New York: Random House, 2000).

2. Jane Tolbert-Rouchaleau, *James Weldon Johnson* (New York: Chelsea House, 1991).

3. Skip Berry, *Gordon Parks: Photographer* (New York: Chelsea House, 1991).

4. James 1:19–20, *NIV and KJV Side-by-Side Bible* (Grand Rapids: Zondervan, 2011).

5. M. W. Taylor, *Harriet Tubman: Antislavery Activist* (New York: Chelsea House, 1991).

Chapter 8: Knowledge

1. Stokely Carmichael, *Stokely Speaks: From Black Power to Pan Africanism* (Chicago: Lawrence Hill Books, 2007).

2. Colin Grant, *Negro with a Hat: The Rise and Fall of Marcus Garvey* (New York: Oxford University Press, 2008).

Chapter 9: Relationships

1. Peter 4:8, *NIV and KJV Side-by-Side Bible* (Grand Rapids: Zondervan, 2011).

Chapter 10: Community

1. Victor Fiorillo, "Trayvon Martin Supporters Want You to Boycott Florida Oranges," *Philly Magazine*, July 15, 2013. https://www.phillymag.com/news/2013/07/15/Trayvon-martin-supporters-boycott-florida-oranges

Chapter 11: Appearance

1. Charlton McIlwain, "Trayvon Martin: The Crime of Being Black, Male, and Wearing a Hoodie," *Christian Science Monitor*, March 27, 2012. https://www.csmonitor.com/Commentary/Opinion/2012/0327/Trayvon-Martin-the-crime-of-being-black-male-and-wearing-a-hoodie/

Chapter 12: Money and Career

1. Robert Hill and Barbara Bair, eds., *Marcus Garvey: Life and Lessons* (Berkeley: University of California Press, 1987).

2. Raymond Smock, *Black Leadership in the Age of Jim Crow* (Chicago: Rowman and Littlefield Publishing Group, 2009).

3. David Levering Lewis, *W. E. B. Du Bois: A Biography 1868–1963* (New York: Holt, 2009).

4. Associated Press, "Suspect in Rosa Parks' Robbery Case Recognized Her, Police Say," *Los Angeles Times*, September 3, 1994. https://www.latimes.com/archives/la-xpm-1994-09-03-mn-34270-story.html

Chapter 13: Health and Well-Being

1. Andrew Glass, "Reagan Declares 'War on Drugs,' October 14, 1982," Politico, October 14, 2010. https://www.politico.com/story/2010/10/reagan-declares-war-on-drugs-october-14-1982-043552

2. Julie Axelrod, "Five Stages of Grief and Loss," Psych Central, July 8, 2020. https://www.psychcentral.com/lib/the-5-stages-of-loss-and-grief

Frequently Asked Questions

How can young Black men build strong character?

How can young Black men support their families?

How can young Black men handle trouble?

What's the connection between spirituality and manhood?

What can make Black men wise leaders?

Dr. Dorrance Kennedy is a graduate of Hampton University. He holds a Doctor of Education (EdD) from Fayetteville State University and a Master of Social Work (MSW) from Southern University. He is a college professor, licensed clinical social worker, motivational speaker, and ordained minister. He is the founder of Empower Your Purpose, an organization dedicated to transforming individuals, organizations, and communities. He has spoken to a wide variety of audiences throughout the nation.